German Ground Forces
Poland and France
1939-1940

German Ground Forces Poland and France 1939-1940

by

Brian Davis

colour illustrations by

The County Studio

and

Brian Fosten

ALMARK

Almark Publishing Co Ltd London

First Published 1976.

ISBN 0 85524 261 2

Distributed in the U. S. A. by
Squadron/Signal Publications Inc.,
3515, East Ten Mile Road,
Warren, Michigan 48091.

Printed in Great Britain by
Edwin Snell Printers,
Babylon Hill, Yeovil,
Somerset,
for the publishers, Almark Publishing Co. Ltd.
49 Malden Way, New Malden,
Surrey KT3 6EA, England.

Contents

Acknowledgements

All pictures are from the author's own collection.

Introduction

The subject of German military uniforms, and especially those of the Third Reich, is vast. The variations in the range of the basic uniform types, the introduction over a period of years of a multitude of insignia and badges as well as the intricacies of detail, colours and manufacturing processes add to the magnitude of this subject. As a serious study it is far too great to be contained within this book. It has therefore been a deliberate decision on the part of myself and the publishers to limit the scope of this, and other works in this series "The Mechanics of War", to a selected range of clothing, uniform items and equipment worn or used by German ground fighting forces in the field during World War II. Set against the chronological order of major military campaigns I have attempted to relate the reasons for the introduction, design and quality of these uniforms to contemporary military and economic circumstances.

This book will describe and explain the uniforms, clothing and equipment, both official issue and the un-official variations, worn by men of the German Army, Waffen-SS, *Fallschirmjäger* personnel – especially when acting as infantry, – Naval units and shore based Marine Artillery detachments, ethnic German military units and to a certain extent German Police employed in a partial or wholly military role.

The date for the introduction of many items of uniform and equipment can, even now, be established with a fair degree of accuracy. Existing documents orders and dress regulations are still available though most of them are in archives and libraries.

However, hardly any accurate information exists which can pinpoint the exact date when these items ceased to be used. Few are recorded as being discontinued or deliberately withdrawn from use. Most clothing, uniform items and equipment, even after they were superseded by new, and presumably better, introductions, continued to be used until they were worn out beyond servicable use and existing stocks were exhausted.

Added to this was the increasing use by the German forces, in the main during the war years, of captured and surplus material, suitably adapted to conform to their requirements. There was also the practice of wearing or using 'unofficial' items usually made up on a unit basis to meet an immediate need or situation where official issue items were either unavailable or non-existent. All this therefore resulted in the mixing of old and new styles and in some instances of second line troops being issued with obsolete forms of clothing and equipment (photo 2).

So familiar have the sight of the modern military service uniforms become that it is often forgotten that these very items of green, grey, khaki, brown or olive-drab, which are now taken so much for granted evolved from

1. German Army 3.7 cm Pak 3516 anti-tank gun and crew during a pre-war exercise.

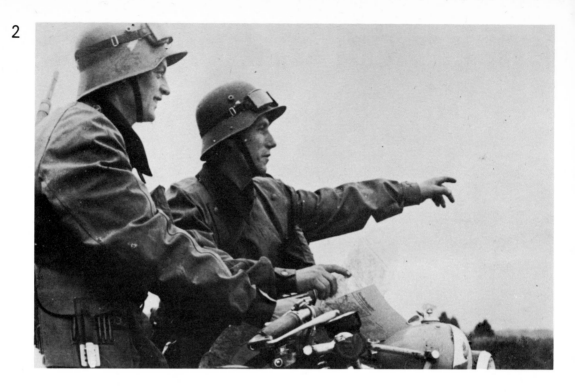

2. Motor cycle dispatch riders in Poland. Despite the model 1935 steel helmet having been standard issue for over four years some second line units and reserve troops were still using the earlier 1918 model.

2

the need for concealment. During World War I the increased range, rapidity and accuracy of fire from every kind of weapon meant that personal concealment for the fighting troops as much as protective trenches and deepbunkers, became of paramount importance. The soldier had no longer to actually stand and face the enemy. Heavy artillery, trench mortars, machine guns and aircraft enabled gun crews to kill and maim their victims at long ranges often without seeing the results of their work. By 1918, when the war had finally ground to its ghastly end, all the belligerents in an attempt to conceal their men, had long since relinquished their elaborate pre-war uniforms and multi-coloured insignia and adopted simple, univer-sally dull-coloured clothing, which conserved material and could be mass produced easily.

Even before the war Britain and her Empire Forces had worn khaki. Italy had adopted a soft grey-green. France quickly learnt the need for survival and clothed her troops in uniforms of dull 'horizon blue'. The Americans arrived in France wearing olive-drab, Russian troops wore khaki brown and the Austro-Hungarian forces started the war wearing pike-grey but, like her ally Germany, eventually chose a universal colour for the uniforms of their respective armies that was a mixture of green and grey known as 'field-grey' (feldgrau).

Between the Wars

Undefeated in the field the 'old' military machine of Imperial Germany was finally broken on 7 May 1919 when the Allied surrender terms were announced. The German Army was to be reduced to a maximum strength of a mere 100,000 men. This was a mortal blow to an army that only six months after the armistice of 1918 still had half a million effective fighting troops and more drastic when it is recalled that in the last months of World War I Germany had been able to put into the field the massive total of 240 divisions.

On 28 June 1919 Germany signed the Treaty of Versailles. The National Army of Germany was reduced to 96,000 men and 4,000 officers. Its overall strength was to be maintained at this level and its composition was carefully prescribed. Men were recruited for 12 year periods of enlistment and new officers were engaged to serve for 25 years. These long service requirements were intended to prevent the accumulation of a large trained reserve of manpower capable of being quickly called up into a much larger army.

Under the Weimar Republic troops of the *Reichsheer*, like their predecessors of 1914-18, wore uniforms of field-grey. But unlike their predecessors their tunics, insignia and medals, in keeping with the attitude of the new Republic, were deliberately subdued, redesigned or abolished. This was an attempt to minimise the 'glorification of war' and counter moves to preserve the German military tradition.

One of Hitler's most telling electioneering posters showed foreigners smashing German guns and burning the prized regimental colours of certain famous German units. He plastered every town and village with statistics showing Germany's losses under the Treaty; 60,000 heavy guns, 130,000 machine guns, 6,000,000 rifles, 16,000,000 bombs, 16,000 planes, 26 capital ships, 23 cruisers, 83 torpedo boats, 315 U-boats and so on.

Ever since coming to power in January 1933 Hitler had fought for German military equality with other European nations and the abolition of the limitation Treaties. For two years he preached an endless campaign for 'equality', working the nation into a frenzy of belief in his foreign policy. Then, when the moment was ripe, he announced the thunderclap of a coup – the reintroduction of military conscription on 16 March 1935.

The 'Law for the Reconstruction of the National Defence Forces' provided that all men of military age had to serve in the army for a year (increased in August 1936 to two years). The existing seven divisions that made up the *Reichswehr* was to be expanded to 36 Army divisions grouped into twelve Army Corps. The name *Reichswehr* was to be abolished and in future all the Armed Forces of Germany were to be known as the 'Wehrmacht' (Defence Force), of which the Army –

3

3. German and
Austrian generals
review a march past
of the 10th Infantry
Division in Vienna
during the
annexation of
Austria in March
1938.

das Heer – was only one part[1].

The expansion from 7 to 36 divisions represented an increase from 100,000 to over 600,000 troops[2]. In order to improve the prospect of a career in the new enlarged German Army and to stimulate voluntary enlistment as well as enhancing the image of the Armed Forces, a number of new uniforms were designed and issued throughout the

Wehrmacht. In addition new badges, insignia, awards and equipment were introduced. These changes and innovations are of importance to this and other books in this series, as it was these pre-war uniforms that established the basic pattern of clothing worn by the German soldier for at least the first two years of World War II. Therefore in order to simplify the complexities of the pre-war

4. A soldier and three non-commissioned officers of the *Reichswehr* display the new rank insignia (arm chevrons) and the eagle and swastika helmet insignia. The strips of silver '*litzen*' worn on the tunic cuffs are just two of the twenty four different distinguishing insignia used to indicate skill at shooting. This system of awards was eventually replaced in June 1936 by the Army Marksmanship Lanyards.

uniform development the various important introductions have been listed in chronological order on page 12.

Anyone in the 1930's, who had taken the trouble to read Hitler's '*Mein Kampf*', could not say that they had not been warned. Hitler's aggressive intentions were there for all to see, yet it would seem few took heed of the warnings.

The Führer's much stated governing impulse and broad purpose had been consistent. Rearm Germany and use that might at every possible opportunity for territorial aggrandizement.

By the spring of 1939 German rearmament, universal military conscription, the reoccupation of the Rhineland, the return of the Saar, the Austrian *Anschluss*, the settlement of the Sudetenland crisis, the occupation of Bohemia-Moravia and the 'Home Coming' of Memel, together with Hitler's intention to settle the question of '*Lebensraum*' within the next few years, made it clear that new aggressive moves were a certainty. Yet the attack on

Item introduced:	Date:
National (cap) Cockade	15.3.1933
Experimental Field Uniform, Steel Helmet etc.	1933
National Emblem (on steel helmet)	17.2.1934
M.1935 Steel Helmet	1935
Special Black Panzer Uniform	3.1935
Grey uniforms for the Waffen-SS	1935
Full Dress Army Uniform Tunic	29.6.1935
Marksmanship Lanyards	29.6.1936
Field-grey Field Service uniforms for the Waffen-SS	1937
Officer's white Summer Undress Tunic	9.7.1937
Army Officer's full dress Parade Belt	8.1937
New style Army Officer's Field Service Cap	6.12.1938
Mouse-grey standard pattern Collar Patches	1939
Mountain Troop *Edelweiss* Cap Badge	2.5.1939
Mountain Troop *Edelweiss* Arm Badge	2.5.1939

5

Poland came as a shock to the world.

Hitler believed that like Czechoslovakia the territories of eastern Europe could be invaded with impunity. The success of the Czech venture had left Poland half surrounded by German territory and relatively helpless. If the acquisition of 'Living Space' in eastern Europe was a prime objective, then Poland was the logical target. Hitler knew that his expansionist policies would inevitable mean war with Britain and to attack France or the Low Countries in 1939 would certainly invite British intervention. It was doubtful if military success in the west could have been achieved by a quick decision and, whilst wanting a military triumph over Poland, the Führer did not want, and could ill afford, a general European war in 1939. Appreciating that the Polish problem was inseparable from conflict with the west, Hitler made every effort to isolate Poland and restrict the fighting to her territory, confident that Britain and France could do nothing to help Poland and little to harm Germany in a short 'Blitzkrieg' war. The German leader reasoned that with a swiftly concluded victory over Poland he could then confront the western powers with a *fait accompli*. At the same time he would seek peace and endeavour to discourage the Allies from continuing a war which would, by that time, look highly unpromising and at the best bloody, costly and protracted.

The decision to attack Poland in 1939 was scheduled for late August or early September. This was late enough in the year to allow sufficient time for full military preparations to take place and time enough to gather in the harvest, but still early enough to ensure a decisive victory before the onset of the mud and fog of late autumn.

The First Victories

Operation White (*Fall Weiss*), the German attack on Poland was launched during the early hours of the morning of Friday 1 September 1939. German forces crossed the Polish frontier in strength advancing from the west and the north[3]. There was no formal declaration of war, the first indication of the outbreak of hostilities were German air attacks on Polish towns.

Germany employed practically every branch of her Armed Forces in overwhelming numbers for the attack. The Luftwaffe, which opened the campaign, bombed and straffed Polish units, fortifications, emplacements and towns. Warsaw, the capital, suffered repeated almost continuous air raids. Panzer units struck swift and deep into Polish territory, supported by artillery and motorised infantry. German paratroops made their appearance, albeit a brief one, during the fighting and the Waffen-SS fought their first actions during the campaign. The battleship *Schleswig-Holstein* supported by other naval vessels was employed in the bombardment of the Polish fortress of Westerplatte and naval personnel from these ships made up shore parties after the fortress surrendered[4]. German Police were used to police the occupied territory, guard prisoners and eventually round up suspected and wanted persons.

German forces began the invasion of Denmark and Norway on 9 April 1940. The attack followed British naval mine laying operations off the Norwegian coast which the Germans regarded as a threat to their shipments of iron ore from Sweden to Germany via Narvik.

Denmark was conquered in a day. While troops crossed the border into Jutland, a battalion of infantry, hidden in a merchantman tied up in Copenhagen harbour, landed to seize the capital with the King and government.

The seaborne attack on Oslo ran into trouble when Norwegian shore batteries sunk the heavy cruiser *Blücher* as she entered Oslo fjord and damaged the pocket battleship *Lützow*. The cruiser *Karlsruhe* had been torpedoed and sunk off Kristiansand.

The OKW had to put together a plan at very short notice when Hitler demanded the invasion of Norway and Denmark. They broke it down into five simultaneous landings. Group I was to take Narvik, Group II Trondheim, Group III Bergen, Group IV Kristiansand and Group V Oslo.

The landings of Groups II, III and IV were successful, but at Oslo the seaborne forces had to disembark on the east shore of the fjord and advance overland to link up with the six companies of German paratroops who had been dropped to capture the airport. At Narvik there was a protracted action with British, French, Norwegian and Polish troops. German sailors whose ships had been sunk in the naval actions in Narvik fjord were employed as infantry and there were parachute drops to

5. An artillery observation officer from the SS Regiment 'Germania'.

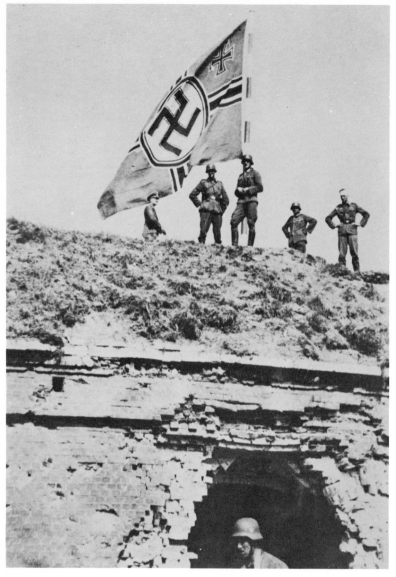

6. The fall of the Westerplatte fortress 7 September 1939.

which, on 7 June 1940, made it necessary to withdraw the Allied Expeditionary Force.

The German forces deployed two Army Corps for Operation *Weserübung,* the XXI for Norway and the XXXI for Denmark. Two Mountain troop divisions were used in Norway and five Infantry divisions, the 29th, 163rd, 181st, 196th, and the 214th with the 170th and 198th in Denmark. An Air Corps, the X *Fliegerkorps,* and every serviceable warship in the German Navy protected 41 troop, weapon and fuel transports.

German losses were 5,636 killed and missing.

While the Polish army was being routed and destroyed in the east, the Franco-British forces did little in the west. A few French divisions advanced five miles but made no attempt to penetrate the Siegfried Line. Even before the gallant Poles were defeated the French had ordered their forces back behind the Maginot Line, the 'Shield of France'. The winter of 1939-40 proved to be the coldest for half a century and while the opposing forces froze behind their fortified positions the Phoney War dragged on.

Between them the British and the French had deployed 87 divisions with a further 36 held in reserve and the neutral Dutch and Belgians added a further 26 divisions. Opposing them the Germans mustered 136 divisions with 2,700 armoured vehicles against the 3,000 of the Allies.

These differences in numbers however were to be more than made up by the modern equipment and aggressive tactics employed by the Germans and their considerable air superiority, 2,000 bombers against 800 and 4,000 fighters against 2,500.

On 10 May 1940 the Germans launched their long awaited offensive, 'Fall Gelb'. Troops from the 6th and 18th Armies of Army Group B under the command of Generaloberst Fedor von Bock attacked

reinforce the hard pressed mountain troops. Eventually the Allies captured Narvik on 28 May and would have forced the German troops over the border into neutral Sweden but for the larger events happening in France

7

Rundstedt advanced into Belgium.

The attack began with a spectacular airborne invasion of neutral Holland. The speed of the attack stunned the Dutch and large numbers of their soldiers were swiftly taken prisoner. The 7th Airborne Division and the 22nd Infantry Air Landing Division were used, troops from the latter were landed around the Hague but suffered heavy losses even though the airfields having been secured by paratroops. Farther south in Belgium the Germans scored another spectacular success in the early hours of the second day of the invasion. The Belgian fort of Eben Emael, considered to be the strongest and most modern of its kind in Europe and the linch pin of the 'Gamelin Line' was swiftly overcome by a glider borne attack of combat engineers from Assault Unit 'Koch'. The airborne engineer

7. Generaloberst Eduard Dietl the Hero of Narvik. Dietl was the first German officer of the Wehrmacht to receive the award of the Knights Cross to the Iron Cross (July 1940).

8. Adolf Hitler with the Paratroop officers who took the Belgium forts at Eben Emael.

8

Holland and Belgium while the men of the 4th, 12th and 16th Armies of Army Group A, commanded by Generaloberst Gerd von

9. The 'Race to the Sea' took its toll of men and machines. An exhausted German tank crew man takes a short rest during a lull in the fighting.

unit commanded by Oberleutnant Rudolf Witzig landed by glider on top of the forts. Blasting their way in with shaped charges and flame throwers they quickly neutralized the nine emplacements of the Eben Emael complex. They achieved their objective in a matter of hours and at the cost of only 6 dead and 15

wounded. Thus the 'Gamelin Line' was breached even before any Allied troops had arrived. General Gamelin had moved 40 of his best divisions, almost half his total strength – including the whole of the British Expeditionary Force, supported by Allied air cover – north into Belgium and Holland. They were moving straight into a well prepared German trap.

The Luftwaffe attacked over 50 British and French airfields on the first day. They destroyed large numbers of aircraft, many of which were still on the ground. The Panzers penetrated deep into the Ardenes, considered by the Allied Command as poor tank country, and by the third day of the offensive they had reached Sedan with its weak French garrisons strung out along the River Meuse. On 12 May all of the bridges over the Meuse had been blown by French engineers, all except one. An old weir some 40 miles north of Sedan had been left intact for fear that destroying it would have lowered the water level so much that the river could be forded. But the French made the error of having left it lightly guarded, as Rommel was quick to discover and exploit.

General Gamelin refused to believe that the Germans could mount a full scale crossing of the Meuse for at least another three to four days. The French generals were pre-occupied with the events happening in Belgium and Holland, and the French artillery dug in on the west bank of the Meuse restricted their firing for fear of expending all their ammunition before the battle proper began. Then the Luftwaffe launched a series of massive Stuka attacks on Sedan, German tanks moved in to destroy the French positions almost at will, and as suddenly as it had begun the bombardment lifted. The German infantry in their rubber assault boats began to cross the Meuse. Incredibly day four of the offensive saw not only the German infantry across the river in strength but German pioneers bridging the river at Dinant, Monthermé and Sedan in readiness for the tanks to cross.

When the French launched counter attacks on the bridgehead they were poorly organized and seldom fully pressed home. French tanks

were prone to mechanical failure and often had to be left behind on the battle field. Massed German tanks now began 'The Race to the Sea'.

The German infantry divisions began to catch up with the Panzers at the Meuse crossing points. For the Germans all was going according to plan. The B.E.F., far to the north in Belgium, had seen little serious fighting but the battle was now virtually decided. Holland surrendered on 14 May, the Dutch having lost 2,100 killed and 2,700 wounded. On the same day the R.A.F. sustained their highest ever losses in aircraft. The most crucial phase of the entire German battle plan began with the swing north to the coast intended to trap the whole of the Allied forces in Belgium.

British troops were immediately ordered back from Belgium, and on 17 May Brussels fell to the Germans. The 68 year old General Gamelin was replaced as Commander-in-

10. Although outnumbered by the Allied AFV's German armour was faster and better controlled. In just seven days the German Panzers had fought their way across 200 miles of French countryside, reaching the Channel coast at Noyelles on 20 May 1940.

Chief of the French Forces by 73 year old General Wegand, hurriedly recalled from virtual retirement. Marshal Petain, aged 84, was appointed Deputy Prime Minister of France. Though the French generals tried to stop the German advance the Panzer commanders always seemed to be one jump ahead of their enemies. In just 7 days the tanks had advanced 200 miles and on the 20 May they reached the Channel coast at Noyelles.

Now the best of the Allied armies in Belgium were cut off from the south. Belatedly the French tried to force a way through to them, but their attack was too weak. On 21 May the British launched an attack at Arras in a vain attempt to break the encirclement but the Germans relentlessly closed in on the Allied troops. Hitler issued his now famous 'Halt Order' to his tanks on the Aa Canal on 24 May and left the reduction of the Dunkirk pocket to the infantry and Göring's Luftwaffe. Events moved rapidly. On 25 May Boulogne fell, two days later Calais, and on 28 May Arras capitulated and the Belgians surrendered. But the Dunkirk perimeter, although much reduced, still held. By 4 June the Royal Navy, with the gallant assistance of many civilian volunteers manning the fleet of little ships, had somehow managed to evacuate 338,226 men from the open beaches of Dunkirk.

When Dunkirk finally fell, Hitler ordered the church bells to be rung throughout the Reich for three days to celebrate what he described as the greatest German victory ever.

The second phase of the Battle for France, or 'Fall Rot' as the German planners called it, began on 5 June.

The armies of von Bock and von Rundstedt had regrouped along the Somme and Aisne. Army Group B launched its attack on 5 June and Army Group A followed four days later. The French, now outnumbered by over two to one fought stubbornly and more aggressively than they had at any time during the battle for the Meuse. Rommel reached the Seine near Rouen on the 8-9 June. On 10 June the French government left Paris and on that same day Mussolini brought Italy into the war on the side of the Axis.

Four days later Paris fell and on the 15 June Marshal Petain, now the Premier of France, following the resignation of Paul Renaud, asked the Germans for an armistice. Hitler insisted on using Marshal Foch's old railway carriage for the negotiations. It had been preserved in the forest at Compiègne where the 1918 armistice had been signed 21 years earlier. It was the supreme humiliation for France. The German triumphal parade took the exact route of the French victory procession held after World War I. It had taken the Wehrmacht just five weeks to humble their historic foe. Denmark, Norway, the Netherlands, Belgium, Luxemburg and now half of France was theirs. They had lost 27,074 men killed, 111,034 wounded and 18,384 missing. The missing were mostly dead, since France, Belgium and Holland were obliged to return their prisoners of war.

Compared with German losses in World War I these were trifling figures weighed against the vast territorial gains. Who in Germany could now doubt the Führer's ability to wage war? Successes like these were to drive Hitler to attempt even greater conquests. But the subsequent cost in men and material was to rise immeasurably.

Uniforms– their Origin and Purpose

The rationale and purpose underlying the use of the German military uniform can be defined as follows:

1. It distinguished its wearer, setting him apart from the rest of the population.
2. Its use created cohesion amongst the troops by developing an esprit de corps, a group mentality not found with civilian clothing.
3. In the 'modern' German Wehrmacht the military uniform went a long way in breaking down old barriers of class distinction.
4. The wearer of the military uniform gave the public a visible reminder of the Armed Forces' strength.
5. By the use of visible indications of rank and power within the Armed Forces internal discipline was maintained and the leadership structure achieved.
6. Due to the conspicuous differences in rank and coverted distinctions, members of the Armed Forces were stirred to ambitions of promotion and achievement.

The study of military uniforms seldom acknowledges the all important role of the designer and artist, the scientist, chemist and manufacturer, all of whom are responsible to some degree for the development of the basic material, the design of the uniform and for its final production. Modern military uniforms don't just happen. They are the result of a tremendous amount of thought, planning, research, testing, organization and hard work. The need to clothe and equip an army is governed by a number of fundamental factors and influenced by a combination of other considerations. These factors and considerations applied to the German Armed Forces just as much as they did (and still do) to any other military force.

To produce the uniforms to clothe the Armed Forces it was necessary that:

1. Suitable machinery and a large enough skilled workforce was available to manufacture the necessary quantity of garments and items.
2. The quality and appearance of the uniforms, taking into consideration differences in rank, had to be carefully controlled throughout its period of production.
3. Individual garments had to be manufactured to a standard that would meet with, and stand up to, the rugged conditions that could be encountered by the troops.
4. The production of the uniforms had to be flexible enough to cope with the variations in size and height of individual soldiers.
5. The cost of the production to the State had to be realistic.
6. The distribution of the uniforms had to be efficient. This was a function usually undertaken by a military department charged with this task and set up within the framework of the Armed Forces.

11. Troops from the 3rd Infantry Division on a pre-war military exercise.

deletion during the war years. Items of uniform which could be privately purchased – usually garments of superior quality that were available to officers, had to conform to the colour, style and cut of the regulation issue item.

Factories operated throughout the Reich producing, under contract to the German Armed Forces, every type of material needed for the manufacture of garments from camouflage shelter quarters, gas capes, uniforms of every sort, clothing, underwear, boots, gloves, hats, steel helmets right down to bullion braiding, badges and buttons. The purchase, control of quality, distribution and sale of items was handled in the German Army by the *Heeres Bekleidungs Amt* – the Army Clothing Office. The German Air Force, Navy, Waffen-SS and Police also had their own clothing offices fulfilling similar functions. Orders relating to every aspect of dress and clothing were periodically issued to all units through handbooks which set out, in one complete edition, dress and equipment regulations in operation at the time of publication. Interim instructions were promulgated through weekly orders published in broad sheet form and circulated from the high commands of the respective services to their individual units throughout the sphere of German military operations.

In addition to these production conditions, two other factors influenced the design and quality of the uniforms worn by the German ground forces before and during the first two years of World War II. In two words these influences can be summed up as 'Climate' and 'Campaigns'.

Pre–war National Socialist Germany was a country whose frontiers extended along the Danish border, the North Sea and the Baltic coasts in the north, the Swiss and Austrian borders in the south, reaching along the frontiers with Poland and Czechoslovakia in the

In addition to the practical requirements in the manufacture of the uniform, traditional and historical features, considered important for the morale of the wearer, were included at the design stage. Where these were practical they were incorporated into the uniform design but were often subject to alteration or

east and France, Luxemburg, Belgium and the Netherlands in the west. Since the end of World War I, East Prussia, an integral part of the German state had been separated by the 'Polish Corridor'. This was a strip of land covering much of what had once been West Prussia which had been taken from Germany by the Allies and given to Poland under the Treaty of Versailles. This gave the land locked Poles access to the Baltic Sea.

Temperatures encountered in Germany were, and still are, very much like those in the British Isles. Conditions range from hot during the summer to wet, misty, cold and even freezing during the winter, but summer or winter, temperatures seldom reach extremes.

These climatic conditions, with their seasonal changes, had an important influence on Germany military uniforms. Generations of German troops have fought over European soil and with the natural progression of historical development and changes in styles, the uniforms that came to be worn by the soldiers of the new Wehrmacht were well suited to European conditions[5].

12. Troops from German units which had participated in the battles around Warsaw parade before the Führer in the Polish capital, 3 October 1939.

13

13. The Model 1935
steel helmet.

14. The Model 1918
steel helmet.

14

Added to the historical development and the climatic conditions influencing the German uniforms were the military circumstances that had prevailed ever since the reoccupation of the Rhineland.

Until Germany attacked Poland all of her territorial expansions had been swift and bloodless. Even the overriding attitude governing the attack on Poland was one of speed. The Blitzkrieg allowed no time for change, let alone development in uniforms.

The German forces that went to war in 1939 wore the uniforms with which they had been issued during the years of peace and which had been introduced from 1936 onwards. Officers tended to wear tailor made uniforms, purchased at their own expense, but when in action wore issue uniforms purchased from their unit stores. Some of these uniform items remained in use for the duration of the war, others survived unchanged for just a few years. However, most were subject to alteration and modification, usually through the need to conserve material and cut back on the labour time required to produce the finished article.

The M.35 Steel Helmet

The steel helmet issued throughout the entire German Armed Forces was the M35, introduced – as its designation indicates – in 1935. This was a development of the experimental helmet first seen two years earlier. (Photo 15). Much lighter and more compact than the earlier 1918 model (Photo 14) this helmet was issued with a grey-green finish. The lining and adjustable chin strap were of leather, the strap usually being dyed black on the outer surface. Helmet insignia for the different branches of the Armed Forces including the German Police varied in design but most of these designs were of approximately the same size and usually placed in the corresponding position on the respective helmets.

15. The experimental prototype steel helmet introduced in 1933 and from which the M.35 helmet was developed.

16. Army helmet insignia.

17. Waffen-SS helmet insignia.

18. SS-Police Division 8-cm mortar crew in action in France, 1940. The helmet insignia worn by these troops was the same as that worn by Police troops.

The M.36 Tunic and Trousers

With the exception of specialist uniforms and clothing the Model 1936 service tunic and trousers was the basic uniform worn by the German soldier at the beginning of the war, and until 1940 remained unchanged (Photo 22). The M36 tunic, together with the field-grey trousers or breeches, the steel helmet, the soft field cap, marching boots, waist belt and equipment (see page 65) made up the basic issue uniform worn both as a service uniform and for field-service use by NCO's and soldiers of the Army and the Waffen-SS, only the insignia distinguishing the troops of the two forces. (Photo 21).

The trousers to the M36 uniform had originally been of a bluish-grey hue but at the beginning of the war the colour had been changed to field-grey to match that of the tunic. Germany had been dependent on foreign sources for the chrome salts required to produce the dye for these blue-grey trousers and this, coupled with the huge increase in demand, as early as 1933, for Army cloth, had strongly influenced the change to vat dyed field-grey material.

19. The funeral parade held at the church of la Madeleine in Paris for the assassinated German officer Hauptmann Scheben. The flag covered coffin is carried by Army NCO's and escorted by Army officers. It is of interest to note that the officer on the right is wearing the issue quality field service tunic with officer's insignia added.

20. Convalescent soldiers take their leave of a nurse. They are wearing the M.38 Other Ranks Field Service Cap (*Feldmütze*).

A German Army motorcyclist dressed in the special rubberised full length coat, water proof gloves and a 1935 pattern steel helmet. The coat could be gathered in around the ankles to give the rider more protection in bad weather.

Two German Army engineers pause as infantry cross a temporary bridge. The engineers are distinguished by the black *waffenfarbe* (arm colour) on their *feldmützen* (field caps) while the infantry have white *waffenfarbe*. There was a comprehensive scheme of colours to cover all the arms of the German Armed Forces.

21. The M.1936 Service tunic was basically the same for both the Army (21) and the Waffen-SS (22). Only the insignia distinguished between these two branches.

23

24. The Officer's Old Style Field Service Cap was one of the few items of German Army and Waffen-SS dress for which there was known to be an exact date for its withdrawal from service. First introduced before the war it was intended to be worn until 1 April 1942, but it proved to be so popular that it continued in use until the end of the war.

25. The *Bergmütze*, or Mountain Cap, was worn by all members of Army Mountaintroop and Ski-Jäger units. It was based on the design of the former Austrian Army service cap and was often worn in preference to all other forms of permitted head-dress. It carried the metal Edelweiss emblem (introduced on 2 May 1939) on the left side. Photo shows Knights Cross holder Oberfeldwebel Wriedt talking to members of the Hitler Youth in his home town of Trier.

23. The *Schirmmütze* (Uniform Peaked Cap) was a form of head-dress universally worn by all ranks in the German Army, the Waffen-SS, the German Police and the Luftwaffe. Although the basic shape and manufacture was the same, the colouring and insignia varied from branch of service and between groups of ranks. It was issued as a dress cap but it was often worn in the field as part of the officer's service uniform when the steel helmet was not required to be worn. The photo shows Oberst (Colonel) Jordan, holder of the Knights Cross. Of interest are the cloth covers used to camouflage the shoulder straps.

25

Two men of the *Panzerwaffe* (tank arm) dressed in their special black uniforms. One man is holding the old style beret while the other is wearing the newer issue field cap. Their uniform has the pink *waffenfarbe* of the armoured forces with the death's head badge on the lapels.

An Oberleutnant of the paratroops briefs a
paratrooper. The paratrooper is dressed in a
splinter pattern smock and is wearing the side
lacing boots issued to airborne forces. Paratroopers
were a Luftwaffe arm and so their rank badges
and insignia were those of the air force.

A The Special Parade
Tunic for Infantry
Regiment
'Grossdeutschland',
here shown for a
private soldier.

B The collar insignia
for an officer.

C The cuff-facing
patches for an
officer.

D The shoulder strap
with 'GD' monogram
as worn by other
ranks.

E The cuff-facing
patches, cuff rank
braiding and
'Grossdeutschland' cuff-
title worn by an NCO
of the rank of
Hauptfeldwebel. The
cuff-title shown here
was of the same
design and worn in
the same position on
the right cuff by all
ranks of the
regiment.

Special Parade Tunic for Infantry Regiment 'Grossdeutschland'

Infantry Regiment 'Grossdeutschland' was an army unit formed before the war as an élite infantry regiment. Unlike other army regiments and divisions whose personnel were normally recruited from within a district or a separate geographic region, volunteers enlisting in Infantry Regiment 'Grossdeutschland' were deliberately drawn from all over Germany. This form of recruitment created a strong feeling of unity within the regiment. Their sense of pride was emphasised by the regimental title 'Greater Germany.'

As a visible expression of this regimental pride a specially designed uniform jacket was proposed for the members of the regiment. It was officially introduced in March 1939, and was to be worn throughout the regiment from 15 September 1939. The uniform tunic was unique in German military sartorial art of this period. It incorporated features adopted from the uniforms of the former *Garde Schützen Bataillon* and the *2.Garde-M.G. Abteilung* as well as the élite regiments of the old Imperial States. These features helped to strengthen the feeling the new regiment had with the traditions of the old Imperial German Army of 1914. However the outbreak of the war overtook the universal issue of the tunic with the result that only those tunics that had been manufactured and issued before September 1939 were actually brought into use and further issues were suspended for the duration.

After September 1939 a proposal was submitted that this elaborate parade tunic should be converted for field use by the removal of the silver collar and cuff-facing *litzen*, and the incorporation of hidden pockets into the skirt of the tunic. However no photographic evidence has come to light − if indeed it ever existed − to show what these converted tunics would have looked like and whether they were ever brought into service.

The illustrations on these pages show the original parade tunic for other ranks, NCO's and officers of Infantry Regiment 'Grossdeutschland' with a projection as to the appearance of the tunic converted for field use.

The members of the regiment went to war in 1939 wearing the normal issue uniform with the model 1936 tunic. Their only distinguishing insignia being the original silver on green 'Grossdeutschland' cuff-title (later changed to silver on black '*Inf. Regt. Grossdeutschland*' and then to silver on black '*Grossdeutschland*') and their monogrammed 'GD' shoulder straps.

A

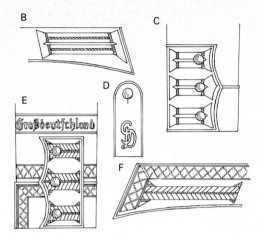

The Greatcoat and Leather Coat

All German troops were issued with a greatcoat, regardless of their rank, branch of service and their individual military role. Officers were permitted to purchase a greatcoat for their own use, usually of better quality than was the case with the regulation issue garment.

The design of this coat was the same for all branches of the Armed Forces[6] only the basic colour distinguished the Army and Waffen-SS (field-grey) from the Luftwaffe (blue-grey) and these two services from the Navy (dark navy-blue).

The colour of the buttons varied, rank insignia was displayed by the wearing of shoulder straps and in the case of Army generals and the equivalent ranks in the Waffen-SS, Air Force and Navy the colour of the greatcoat lapel facings varied.

The greatcoat was a garment which proved perfectly adequate to protect the wearer from the cold weather normally encountered in Germany and Europe. Extremes of cold weather such as to be found in Russia were too much for the troops and the greatcoat failed to afford sufficient protection.[7]

Raincoats did exist in the German Armed Forces but their use was very limited and they were only worn by officers. They so closely resembled the greatcoat other than those worn by generals both in design and colouring that from a distance it was almost impossible to distinguish the raincoat from the greatcoat.

Coats manufactured from fine quality leather and cut to conform to the design of the military cloth greatcoat were available to be purchased by officers of the Armed Forces as an extra item and at their own expense. Although they were an expensive item for an officer to buy they proved to be a popular, hardwearing and practical coat which stood

F The collar insignia for an NCO. This consisted of rank braiding and a single length of 'litzen'.

G The Special Parade Tunic converted for field use by the removal of all collar 'litzen' and cuff-facing patches and by the addition of pockets let into the skirt of the tunic.

A military policeman of the *Feldgendarmerie* with a soldier of the Waffen–SS. The military policeman has the duty gorget hung around his neck which earned the pejorative nick name *ketten hund* "chained dogs".

Men of the *Gebirgstruppen* (mountain troops) dressed in camouflaged anoraks and trousers. During the invasion of Norway German troops had to make do with extemporised white camouflage since they had not received these uniforms in time. The soldiers wear the *Bergmütze* (mountain cap), a popular and practical item of headgear.

 27. The Commander-in-Chief of the German Army, Generalfeldmarschall von Brauchitsch wearing leather greatcoat takes the salute at a march past of German Infantry, France May 1941.

up to continuous wear and dirt far better than the issue greatcoat. They were permitted to be worn on all occasions calling for the greatcoat other than official parades and functions.

Officers of the Army, the Waffen-SS and the Police wore coats dyed in a shade of dull green-grey whilst Officers of the German Air Force had leather coats in a blue-grey hue. The only insignia of rank permitted to be worn on these coats were the shoulder straps, although some Waffen-SS Officers added other items of insignia.

26. Prior to the winter warfare in Russia and the introduction in 1943 of heavy duty cold weather clothing, German troops had only their issue greatcoat for wear during cold weather. Soldiers required to stand guard duty during winter were issued with a heavy fleece lined animal skin guard coat. This was usually worn together with woollen gloves, an 'ear protector' – a form of 'Balaclava Helmet' (see also photo number 52) and warm footwear. It should be noted that this form of clothing was not used for combat. It was far too cumbersome to be practical.

28. Soldiers from the School of Artillery acting as gunnery observers. All are wearing the issue greatcoat.

The Rubberised Motor-Cycle Coat

The use of the motor-cycle was very widespread throughout the German Armed Forces and especially within the Army. They in particular possessed reconnaissance units made up of motor-cyclists, either riding on single machines or motor-cycle combinations. Dispatch riders made full use of the motor-cycle. The motor bike was well suited for the job of conveying messages swiftly and at little cost. When ridden by an experienced rider these machines could cross rough country at considerable speed where the conventional four wheeled motor vehicle would find the terrain too difficult. However military motor-cycles had one disdvantage, they afforded little, if any, protection to the rider against wind, cold weather, rain or mud (Photo 29). The

A paratrooper doubles into action in a field grey jump smock with ammunition bandoliers slung around his neck. The smock varied in pattern, but most types included zip pockets and were designed with short trouser legs to prevent the smock billowing up during the parachute descent.

An Oberleutnant of the artillery. He is wearing the Iron Cross First and Second class. His brown belt with double claw buckle is a standard officer's item and his *Schirmütze* has been battered by wear in the field.

German Armed Forces did not use wind-shields on their motor bikes and even their side cars were without passenger screens or covers so riding one during cold or wet weather could be an uncomfortable and miserable experience.

To counter this hazard motor-cyclists were issued with a specially designed heavy duty, rubberized waterproof motor-cycle coat. It was a double breasted, loose fitting garment buttoning down the front with the skirt of the coat reaching to the height of the wearer's calf. The skirt to the coat could be gathered in around the legs and buttoned in position to allow for easier and safer movement whilst riding on the motor bike. There were two large pockets positioned in the front and to each side of the coat, each with a large button-down pocket flap. Army, Waffen-SS, Luft-waffe and Police personnel of motor-cycle units, individual riders and occasionally drivers of vehicles that were exposed to the elements were issued with this coat, the only difference distinguishing one branch of service from the other being either the basic colour of the coat or the colour of the collar facing cloth. The German Army, the Waffen-SS and the Police were issued in coats of field-grey colouring. The cloth facing to the collars varied for the Army and the Waffen-SS being either field-grey or dark blue green. The Police were issued with field-grey coats with collars of field-grey or dark brown, this later colour being worn by their *Gendarmerie* personnel. The Luftwaffe motor-cyclists received blue grey coats with collars in a matching colour cloth[8].

29. Without the protection of leg guards or wind screens German military motor cycle riders could become either wet through or covered in mud. The rubberised motor cycle coat therefore proved a very useful item of clothing.

31. An Army three-man motor cycle unit entering Prague, riding on a BMW R12 745-cc motorbike combination.

30. German Police motor cyclists taking part in the Austrian Anschluss. All are wearing the Police motor cycle coat and gauntlets as well as the distinctive Police Shako.

31

A General wearing the white summer tunic in
conversation with an officer of the General Staff.
The latter is distinguished by the broad red stripes
down his breeches.

Two soldiers of the *Gebirgstruppen*. The man leading the horse is wearing the sage green double breasted coat issued to mountain troops, while the other man is wearing a *Zeltbahn*. Visible on the side of the soldiers' caps is the Edelweiss emblem.

32. German tank crew members in Poland. This Black Uniform, designed especially for use with and inside an armoured vehicle, even had the shoulder straps stitched down onto the shoulders of the jacket to prevent them becoming caught up on any projection inside the vehicle.

33. The Special Black Panzer uniform originally intended for use with the armoured vehicle came to be used as a parade and walking-out uniform.

34. In addition to being issued with a black uniform Panzer troops received a normal issue field-grey uniform. The picture shows an interesting mixture of the black Panzer beret being worn with the field-grey uniform.

The Special Black Panzer Uniform

When before the war a separate Tank arm was first formed a new and special uniform was introduced for wear by the crews of the armoured vehicles. This uniform was a complete departure from the standard issue military uniform in use at that time, both in style and colour. Manufactured from black material the two piece uniform consisted of a jacket and trousers worn together with a grey shirt and black tie. The jacket was short, double breasted, without external pockets and with concealed buttons. The long, slightly baggy black trousers were worn full length

with the ends gathered in around the ankles and folded over the top of the short black leather ankle boots.

This special black uniform was originally intended for wear only when the crews were on duty with their armoured vehicles, a normal field-grey uniform and greatcoat being provided for all other occasions. (Photo 34). However the black uniform became so popular with the armoured troops and proved attractive enough that they took to wearing it with pride for all military and social functions.

As part of this uniform tank and armoured car crews were issued with a black beret, consisting of a crash liner fitted with a beret

cover. The German Panzer beret had been devised no doubt influenced by the French and British experiments in the search for a compact, soft and close fitting head-dress suitable for wear inside an enclosed armoured vehicle. However, the black Panzer beret lasted for only a few years, being gradually phased out even during the Polish campaign[9]. As early as the late summer of 1939 the new black Panzer *feldmutze* had made its appearance and eventually this cap replaced the Panzer beret altogether.

An officer of the self propelled artillery directs the fire of a half track mounted 3.7 cm Flak 18. The uniform is similar to that of the panzer troops, but being field grey it afforded better camouflage to the wearer.

An *Untersturmführer* (2nd Lieutenant) of the
Waffen–SS artillery talks to a soldier of the
Waffen–SS. The soldier is wearing the mottled
smock and helmet cover that was almost a trade
mark of the Waffen–SS.

35. Waffen-SS Panzer troops were issued with a uniform of the same pattern and colour as that issued to Army Panzer personnel. Only their insignia distinguished between the two branches of the armed forces. Photo shows an SS guard contingent on the Franco-Spanish frontier at Hendaye.

36. A close-up view of the crown to the Black Panzer beret showing its short 'tail'.

37. The black Panzer *Feldmütze* both for officers and other-ranks first began to make its appearance during the 1939 Polish campaign. It eventually replaced the Panzer beret as crew head-dress.

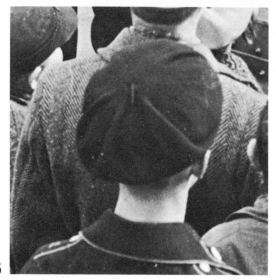

36

The Field-Grey S.P. Gun Uniform

Although the black uniform, with its distinctive beret, proved to be adequate for use within the confines of the armoured vehicles it had the disadvantage that its wearer became very conspicuous when he left the safety of his vehicle and stood in the open. His black uniform was sufficient indication to enemy reconnaissance troops that German armoured units were in their vicinity.

Experience during the Polish campaign had shown that the black uniform afforded little camouflage to the wearer. With the introduction of self-propelled artillery, where

7

8

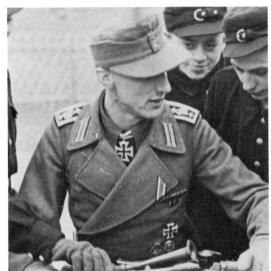

the crews were required to observe either from their vehicles or in advance of their units in the open, it was found necessary to issue a uniform less conspicuous than the special black Panzer uniform.

The extra warmth provided by the double breasted jacket and the lack of external pockets and flaps that eliminated snagging were considered excellent features in the special black Panzer uniform. So while the cut of the uniform was retained, for the sake of better camouflage the colour was changed to field-grey.

38. Oberwachtmeister Kessel, holder of the Knights Cross and a member of the Panzerjäger Abteilung Grossdeutschland wearing the field-grey uniform for assault gun and self-propelled artillery crews.

German Reich, the Austrian Alps. These *Gebirgstruppen* were therefore the obvious choice to take a major part in the attack on, and subsequent occupation, of Norway.

However the winter of 1939-40 was the worst in Europe for 47 years and despite the mountain troops being acclimatized to cold weather conditions they were ill prepared to face these severe extremes of low temperature. No special provision had been made by way of extra warm clothing and they had not received any form of camouflage for the snow covered Norwegian countryside.

39. A member of the *Leibstandarte-SS* "Adolf Hitler" assault gun unit wearing the SS version of the Special Field-Grey uniform.

Mountain Troops

Germany possessed units of troops trained in all forms of mountain warfare. During peacetime their training areas had been the mountains of southern Germany and later, with the incorporation of Austria into the

40. Members of Mountain Troop units who had one year's qualifying experience as a mountain guide were entitled to wear the *Heeres-Bergführer* badge. The badge instituted on 10 August 1936 is shown here being worn above the German Reichs Sports Award Badge on the left breast tunic pocket.

41. Recruits from Mountain Troop units were trained in all forms of mountain warfare including ski-ing and rock climbing as well as infantry and artillery tactics. Although the troops of Mountain Units wore basically the same style uniform as that issued to infantry troops they were distinguished by their Mountain Cap (the *Bergmütze*) their Edelweiss arm and cap badge and when in the field by the use of specialist clothing and equipment for use when climbing and scaling through hilly and mountainous terrain.

42

Naval Landing Rig and extemporised uniforms

In an effort to protect her invasion fleet and supply ships the German Navy committed almost all her warships to the Norwegian campaign. British naval action, bombing and torpedo attacks and fire from Norwegian shore batteries took a heavy toll of the German ships. A number of major vessels were sunk in Norwegian waters and ten destroyers were sent to the bottom with loss of life off Narvik. The German sailors who managed to reach the Norwegian shore were drafted into service with Generaloberst Dietl's hard pressed forces. These German survivors were ill equipped to fight alongside their mountain troop comrades but with the astute use of captured weapons and Norwegian clothing they were able to contribute to the eventual German victory.

43

42. As part of their issue equipment Mountain Troops received heavy duty climbing boots, the soles and heels of which were well protected by cleats and hobs.

43. Gebirgsjäger troops being ferried in rubber assault boats across a Norwegian fjord.

44

45

44. A sailor from a Danzig naval unit and a member of the German Marine Artillery stand guard over Polish soldiers taken prisoner after the fall of the Westerplatte garrison.

45. Naval survivors from sunken German vessels had to make use of whatever clothing was available in order to exist during the bitterly cold Norwegian winter of 1940. Photo shows a sailor wearing a mixture of German and captured Norwegian clothing and equipment.

46. A survivor from the second battle of Narvik is shown here wearing a curious mixture of a naval side cap, snow goggles, Luftwaffe tunic and Norwegian Army trousers.

47. The first German troops to set foot on British soil landed at Jersey airport. German naval and Luftwaffe Staff officers are seen here talking to the Mayor of Jersey. The Naval officers are wearing a modified version of officer's shore landing rig.

Police Troops

Following hard on the heels of the German military, once they had overrun Poland and Western Europe were the German Police. The members of these Police Battalions were drawn from the ranks of the *Schutzpolizei* and they were used to maintain order in the occupied territories. Although they appeared somewhat similar to the German soldiers they did in fact have a special uniform. It was a grey-green M.1936 Police tunic with distinctive dark brown collar and cuffs and police green piping, trousers or breeches, greatcoat, steel helmet, peaked cap or field cap, boots and equipment. They carried weapons including pistols, rifles and sub-machine guns.

48. A German Police patrol in occupied Warsaw inspect the contents of a Polish warehouse.

48

49

50

50a

49. Members of the German *Schutzpolizei* disarm Polish soldiers in Warsaw, October 1939. Although somewhat similar to the German Army tunic the M.36 Police tunic, shown being worn here, had a dark brown collar and cuffs with Police green piping and white metal buttons.

50. Police troops received a *Feldmütze,* identical in shape to that issued to the Waffen-SS. The Police emblem (50a), an eagle and swastika within an oakleaf wreath was displayed on the front of the cap.

51. The *Feldgendarmerie Ringkragen* (Gorget) (a), *Feldgendarmerie* Police arm eagle badge (b) and cuff-title (c).

The *Feldgendarmerie*

The *Feldgendarmerie* was a military body with police powers and part of the German Army in the field. Its members were recruited from the ranks of the *Ordnungspolizei*. Their duties consisted of traffic direction and control duties at ports, aerodromes and railway stations. They were responsible for establishing temporary town majors and army stragglers posts, rounding up of enemy stragglers and terrorists, collecting refugees and prisoners of war, guarding booty and ensuring that weapons in the hands of civilians were surrendered. They were also responsible for the organization of civilian labour and the erection of military and civil road signs. In the home areas of the Reich their task was to ensure discipline amongst troops, round up deserters, control military traffic, marshall refugees and evacuate prisoners.

52. A member of an Army *Feldgendarmerie* unit on traffic control duty wearing the duty gorget over his motor cycle coat.

51a

51b

51c

53

The *Fallschirmjäger*

German paratroops, a specialist force of highly trained troops, came under the command of the Luftwaffe. As such they were issued with both normal Air Force uniforms as well as a number of items of specialist clothing required for their role as paratroopers. When in the field paratroopers wore a specially designed helmet often with a cloth helmet cover. Their uniform consisted of the Luftwaffe blue-grey flying blouse, field-grey trousers of a special cut and calf-length, black leather, side lacing, rubber soled, jump boots. A special jump smock manufactured from either olive green or Army pattern camouflage cotton drill material was worn over the blouse. The leather equipment fitted over the smock and in general it was the same as that used by an infantry soldier. The gas mask however was carried in a soft canvas case, especially designed to prevent injury to the wearer on landing from an air drop. Paratroopers carried additional rifle ammunition in cloth bandoliers consisting of several compartments designed to take ammunition clips. These bandoliers were hung around the neck, with the compartments lying flat against the soldier's chest (Photo 53).

53. A paratrooper on sentry duty wearing both the standard issue leather ammunition pouch and the cloth bandolier for rifle ammunition clips.

54. The green splinter-pattern camouflage paratroop jump smock.

55. The Luftwaffe Flying Blouse, grey-green paratroop trousers, uniform peaked cap, shirt, tie and boots was normal issue to German Paratroopers.

56. A paratrooper wearing a helmet with the camouflaged cover.

56

57. The Fall of Rotterdam. General Kurt Student congratulates his men who took part in the airborne assault on the Dutch city.

Camouflage Clothing and the Zeltbahn

The German Army had considered camouflage of major importance for a long time before World War II and undertaken research for a number of years. In 1932 a camouflage pattern was adopted by the Army for general use. It became a standard pattern, but there were some later modifications. As first conceived the printed design had sharp, distinct lines between the colours. Later this was altered so that the lines were less distinct and the edges of each colour were irregular and tended to merge. Still later, during the course of the war, this pattern was again modified to produce an even more blurred effect with one colour blending into another. Some changes

58. The issue Zeltbahn being worn here as a rain cape by Army artillery troops.

in colour combinations were also introduced.

The *zeltbahn* – the German waterproof shelter triangle – was the most common item of camouflage equipment issued universally throughout the German Army, Waffen-SS, Luftwaffe and later the Luftwaffe Field Divisions[10]. Its use was widespread and although it was an item of equipment it was worn as waterproof clothing by all Armed Forces personnel[11] who were required to work, march or fight in wet or damp weather.

The *zeltbahn* was so designed that when worn as a rain cape it could be buttoned around the wearer's body in a number of ways depending on whether the soldier was marching, or riding a horse or bicycle. This flexibility in design allowed for the maximum freedom of movement whilst at the same time providing adequate protection from the rain.

When the *zeltbahn* was used as equipment it provided each soldier with a simple wind break, which when pitched as a rough shelter gave sufficient protection to an individual soldier. The waterproof shelter triangle could also be buttoned to other triangles and if sufficient numbers were available a tent could be constructed large enough for a small group of men to use for shelter or sleeping.

Waffen-SS Smocks and Helmet Covers

Although it was the German Army that had initiated the research in camouflage materials as far back as 1932, it was the Waffen-SS who adopted this innovation and developed it far more extensively than the Army.

As soon as the Waffen-SS was officially established, experiments were conducted with camouflage fabrics and it was soon decided that the Waffen-SS would adopt a camouflage pattern of its own. A number of well known

59. Waffen-SS troops from the SS-Heimwehr Danzig took part in the Polish campaign.

59

60. Men from a Waffen-SS motorised infantry unit. All are wearing the 'Tiger Jacket' and the camouflage cloth helmet cover.

artists, who were considered to be experts in colours and hues, were commissioned to work out the most effective form of camouflage patterning. Many designs were submitted and studied. Certain patterns were put onto cloth to determine their effectiveness. Finally one was selected and adopted by the Waffen-SS. This was the work of Professor Otto Schik who, in working out his patterns and colour combinations, had made a careful study of the effect of sunlight through trees both in summer, when they were in full leaf, and during the autumn, when most vegetation was dried and brown. In this manner he achieved his colour combination and some of the fabrics subsequently produced had a green combination on one side and the brown patterning on the other. This basic patterning used by the Waffen-SS was modified slightly during the course of the war.

Three items of SS camouflage equipment had been developed and tested under field conditions before the war, the SS *zeltbahn*, the helmet cover and the face mask. This last item was however considered unsuitable and was not issued during the early years of the war[12].

The helmet cover and the 'Tiger Jacket' – the M.1939 reversible camouflage smock – both items which had been devised by *SS-Sturmbahnführer* Dr. Ing. Brandt, were issued on a limited scale to SS assault troops and used during both the Polish and French campaigns.

61. The Waffen-SS 'Tiger Jacket' was a smock-like pullover garment manufactured from water-repellent linen duck printed on both sides with a contrasting camouflage patterning. The design on one side was predominantly green for use during the spring and summer whilst the reverse was printed with browns and tans for use during the autumn and winter seasons. Photo shows the smock being worn over the issue greatcoat during cold weather.

Combat Equipment and extemporised camouflage

There are only a limited number of areas on the human frame that will take the strain of load carrying with any degree of comfort whilst at the same time affording freedom of movement. The most obvious of these are the hands and arms. The shoulders, the back, the waist and to a certain extent the forehead can be used and it was on this principle that the

personal equipment worn by the ordinary infantryman were designed. When fully assembled and correctly worn this equipment allowed the soldier to carry, with the minimum of effort, the basic necessities of food, water, clothing, tools and ammunition sufficient for his survival in the field for a limited period of time.

The leather waist belt was the anchor upon which other items of equipment were hung or fixed. A set of leather straps helped to support

62. A signaller from an Army Signals Instruction school operating a field telephone whilst wearing his gas mask. When not in use the gas mask was stowed away in the cylindrical carrying case hung against the small of the soldier's back.

A large variety of personnel equipment was carried throughout the Armed Forces by troops from the various arms of service. Many of these specialist items of equipment were the result of new weapons having been brought into service. However in 1939 and 1940 certain basic items were common issue to most ground forces. These were the black dyed leather waist belt with metal buckle, support 'Y' straps with metal 'D' rings, rifle ammunition pouches, bread bag, water bottle, mess tins, bayonet and scabbard, gas mask canister and gas mask and the entrenching tool in its carrying case.

the waist belt and the equipment hung from the belt. These 'Y' straps so named for their shape passed over the shoulders at the front and met in the centre of the wearer's shoulder blades and were joined to a metal ring with a single strap reaching down to the belt at the back (Photo 64). The range of equipment carried on the belt varied according to the soldier's needs, his military function, or the type of weapon he carried or manned.

Attempts to camouflage metal equipment like steel helmets, mess tins and gas masks with a rough coating of paint are never really successful. Unavoidable nicks, scratches and rubbing soon expose the bright metal finish.

Early attempts had been made to provide camouflage to the helmet. On an individual basis mud was applied to the smooth surface in a crude effort to protect against shine (Photo 67). Even before the start of hostilities the Waffen-SS had realised the advantage of a fabric cover for their helmets. A number of their troops fought in Poland and France wearing covers manufactured from camouflage printed material (Photo 66). The addition of cloth loops stitched to these covers

64

63. An Army non-commissioned officer gives the signal to 'dig in'.

64. The 'D' ringed 'Y' support straps.

65. Infantry wearing the basic issue equipment.

65

66. A Waffen-SS motor cyclist wearing the camouflage smock and helmet cover. The 'leaf pattern' design of camouflage used on the smock was an official variation to the standard SS ragged spot patterning. The helmet cover, whilst completely covering and disrupting the hard outline to the helmet also eliminated shine. It was not until 1942 that the simple expedient of providing additional camouflage for the helmet by means of cloth loops attached to the cover was introduced.

67. Unlike the Waffen-SS the German Army took some time before it adopted a cloth cover for the helmets of their troops. Until then individual soldiers had attempted to disrupt the shiny surface by smearing mud onto the helmet. However this was an unsatisfactory method as it was not a permanent solution to the problem of camouflage.

which enabled the helmet to be garnished with grass and other vegetation were not brought into use until 1942.

Gas mask canisters and mess tins were sometimes wrapped in cloth, which also helped to prevent rattling. During special operations such as reconnaissance patrols and night raids[13] such equipment as entrenching tools, bayonets and binoculars which were liable to make noise, especially when the wearer was running, were also wrapped in cloth.

German officers, and especially Generals were particularly vulnerable to sniper fire. Many

regimental officers quickly learnt to conceal their presence in front line areas by covering their shoulder straps with cloth covers (Photo 23) and dyeing their brown leather belts black, thus denying the enemy identification of their unit and rank.

From the point of view of camouflage the broad red and carmine 'stripes' on the trousers or breeches of Generals and General Staff Officers were extremely undesirable. Whenever possible they were not worn when these officers visited a difficult area. The General's gold and red insignia was also much too conspicuous. As well as inviting

67

assassination by partisans or being shot at by the enemy troops, the appearance of a General could immediately betray the presence and location of a headquarters to the local population and provide unnecessary assistance to spies.

Experience during the trench warfare of World War I had shown that map mounting boards were impractical when used in the front line. When in use they were not only cumbersome and awkward but they could reveal the position of a unit's headquarters to an observant enemy often bringing down enemy artillery or mortar fire on these positions.

Anyone observed carrying or using a free folding map could be considered to be either an officer or at least an NCO in charge of a group of men responsible for controlling their movement. Therefore in an attack or ambush it was essential to kill these people first, thus denying the rest of the troops the leadership they would need. It became evident that these give away maps had to be concealed when not in use and this was done by the provision of large pockets designed into the tunics of the German officer's service uniform.

Leather map cases that could be worn hung from the waist belt or by a single strap hung over the shoulder around the body were also used both by officers and NCO's (Photo 21).

¹ The announcement proclaiming the existence of a third arm of the German forces, the new Luftwaffe, was made at the same time as the reintroduction of military conscription. The Army, German Navy and the Air Force fulfilled the historic role as 'bearers of arms for the German people'. Not until 1942 was the status of the Waffen-SS raised to their same level when it was officially recognised as being the fourth branch of the Wehrmacht. At the celebrations held in Berlin to commemorate 'Heroes Memorial Day' on 15 March 1942 contingents of the Waffen-SS appeared in public for the first time as an independent branch of the Armed Forces, having equal status with the Army, Navy and Air Force. Hitherto the Waffen-SS had formed part of the Army.

² Even this (maximum) figure of 36 divisions as laid down in the Army Law of March 1935 refered only to infantry divisions. It did not take into account, in an effort to deceive foreign critics, the three extra Panzer divisions already in existence at Berlin, Wurzburg and Weimar and the plans for the formation of three more.

³ On the eve of the attack on Poland the total strength of the German Army in the field was about 2,500,000 men, of whom 1,000,000 were in the west and about 1,500,000 in the east. The figures for the troops employed in Operation White were as follows:

Third Army (General Georg von Kuechler)	320,000
Fourth Army (General Gunther von Kluge)	230,000
Army Group North Reserve	80,000
Total Army Group North (Generaloberst Fedor von Bock).	630,000
Eighth Army (General Johannes Blaskowitz)	180,000
Tenth Army (General Walter von Reichenau)	300,000
Fourteenth Army (Generaloberst Siegmund Wilhelm List).	210,000
Army Group South Reserve	196,000
Total Army Group South (Generaloberst Gerd von Rundstedt).	886,000
Grand Total	1,516,000

68. 69. German infantry in Poland. A variety of personal equipment can clearly be seen including the map case, rolled zeltbahn, gas mask canister, mess tins, water bottle and bread bag.

[4] From the first hours of the German invasion the Poles fought fiercely but were outnumbered in troops, guns and aircraft. Polish officials made a brave but vain stand at the Danzig post office and railway station. At the entrance to the harbour of the Free City of Danzig a company of Polish soldiers commanded by Major Koscianski manning the Westerplatte fortress refused to surrender to the Germans. For six days they withstood the furious onslaught of repeated attacks from overwhelmingly superior German land and air forces and continuous point blank bombardment from the 11 inch guns of the battleship 'Schleswig-Holstein.' Not until the morning of 7 September did the survivors of the garrison finally submit.

[5] These uniforms were not suitable, however, for the desert conditions in North Africa nor the severe winters of Russia, subjects which will be dealt with in forthcoming Almark books in this series.

[6] It was the terrible winter of 1941-42, somehow endured by the German troops fighting on the Eastern Front, that showed the need for some other form of warm winter clothing to replace the inadequate greatcoat. This will be covered in another title in this series.

[7] Various modifications were made to the original design of the cloth greatcoat. Later in the war due to economic restrictions new styles of the greatcoat were introduced. These will be covered in future publications.

[8] Lightweight tropical motor-cycle coats were issued to troops in North Africa and other warm climate zones which were of the same basic design as the rubberized version but were manufactured from heavy duty cotton drill in two versions of colouring, olive green drab and dull tan.

[9] The Panzer crash beret made a late comeback towards the end of the war in Europe when remaining stocks were once again issued to troops operating *Panzerwerfer 42* multi-barreled motorized mortars.

[10] Clothing manufactured from camouflaged patterned materials, either of single weight quality for summer use or in camouflage patterns reversible to white for use in snow covered landscapes, were introduced later in the war. Despite the Waffen-SS being issued with specially manufactured camouflaged helmet covers which they wore during the 1939 and 1940 campaigns, the German Army did not take up the idea of helmet covers until the Russian campaign was well under way.

[11] The Waffen-SS were also issued with these shelter quarters which were identical in design to the ones used in the Army but printed in the camouflage patternings peculiar to the Waffen-SS.

[12] The stockpiled quantities of these face masks were eventually released in April 1942 for use by the Waffen-SS serving on the Eastern Front.

[13] For night operations involving possible close combat with the enemy it was advisable for the face and hands of the infiltrating soldiers to be blackened. Tank commanders observing from their turrets should also camouflage their faces. This blackening of the features also helped to distinguish between friend and foe.

Bibliography.
This book by its very size cannot hope to cover every aspect of German uniforms let alone the entire range of clothing, equipment and related insignia for all the German ground forces, even for the limited period from 1939 to 1940. Therefore the following publications are recommended as a source for further reading. At the time of going to press all these books are known to be in print.
Bender, Roger James & Taylor, Hugh Page. *"Uniforms, Organization and History of the Waffen-SS"*. R. James Bender Publishing, California, U.S.A. Vols 1, 2, 3 & 4 various dates 1969-1976.
Davis, Brian L. *"German Army Uniforms and Insignia, 1933-1945"* Arms & Armour Press, London, 1971.
Davis, Brian L. *"German Parachute Forces, 1935-1945"*. Key Uniform Guide number 5, Arms and Armour Press, London, 1974.
Mollo, Andrew. *"German Uniforms of World War II"*. Macdonald & Jane's, London, 1976
Mollo, Andrew. *"Uniforms of the SS"*. Historical Research Unit, London. Vols 3, 4, 6 & 7. Various dates 1970-1976.